Christina Aguilera - Official Web Site: www.christina-a.com

Christina Aguilera - Fan Club Address: Christina Aguilera Official Fan Club
244 Madison Avenue, #314
New York, NY 10016

Project Manager: Carol Cuellar
Book Art Layout: Odalis Soto
CD Artwork © 1999 BMG Entertainment
Photography: Yaariv Milchan

© 2000 WARNER BROS. PUBLICATIONS
All Rights Reserved

Any duplication, adaptation or arrangement of the compositions
contained in this collection requires the written consent of the Publisher.
No part of this book may be photocopied or reproduced in any way without permission.
Unauthorized uses are an infringement of the U.S. Copyright Act and are punishable by law.

christina aguilera

the Music . . . the Lyrics . . . the Album . . . the Artist

I met Christina Aguilera two years ago just as she was about to celebrate her seventeenth birthday. We were brought together by chance—maybe old-fashioned luck, perhaps fate. Bob Jamieson, president of RCA Records, arranged the meeting. Christina was accompanied by her manager, Steven Kurtz. Christina stood two feet away from me in a small office of RCA Records on a winter's day in New York City. This was the moment she had prepared for her entire life—an audition with a major record company. Her dream was coming true. Christina's life was about to change forever.

I asked her to sing. "Right here—right now?" she asked with sassy surprise. "Yes, please. Just sing *a cappella* (with no backing music) if you don't mind. Anything you like." Christina paused for a second. "Did you see *The Preacher's Wife*?" she asked. "This is a song that Whitney sung." She closed her eyes—and took a breath. Fearlessly, she belted out the song—as if she were on stage at Carnegie Hall—powering through complex vocal riffs with a strong personal style, perfect intonation and a tremendous confidence way beyond her age. It was my once-in-a-lifetime meeting with an artist I had always dreamed of—a God-given talent rolled into an all-American girl-next-door, curious, intuitive, emotional and beautiful young star. And so, as the story goes, I called my boss Bob Jamieson and said, "We must put Christina Aguilera under contract to RCA Records right away." There was only one small problem: What songs would Christina sing?

And so we began the process we call "the A&R" of the album. The "A" stands for "artist," and the "R" stands for "repertoire"—the songs. Christina became the "A." The "R" always turns out to be the hard part because there are so many roads to choose—so many directions to go— each song is a key to a door that opens to a musical journey. Christina wanted to sing songs that would show the world her incredible ability—songs she could swoop down upon, leap around and tear up vocally. As her "A&R man," I explained to Christina it was important to carve out a unique collection of songs that would bring the success she deserved, connect with a large worldwide audience and give her a fun musical playground as well. So we reached out to a community of songwriters, producers, engineers, musicians, song-pluggers and friends.

We were flooded with material being pitched by every level of songwriter—unknown newcomers, seasoned professionals, even one of our greatest living songwriters, Diane Warren. More than 150 songs considered did not make the final cut. Christina, her manager Steve Kurtz and I would meet every day and just listen. We would disagree, argue a little, listen some more, discuss and come together on every decision. At the beginning of this journey, Christina didn't quite know where it would lead—putting together her first album for the first time. Soon we built a strong musical trust and the pieces began to fit together. Each one of the songs we chose became like a child that needed nurturing, love and attention. Each one has a unique little back-story, which I would like to share with you.

"Genie in a Bottle" (written by Steve Kipner, David Frank and Pam Sheyne)
I received the demo produced by David and Steve. David was in the band The System and had written "Don't Disturb This Groove." Steve wrote the classic Olivia Newton-John song "Let's Get Physical" and Chicago's "Hard Habit to Break." It took only one listen to "Genie" to know this could be the song to launch Christina into orbit. Christina has been asked a lot about the meaning of "you gotta rub me the right way." "It's a play on words. Rub me the right way is symbolic of treat me the right way," says Christina. "Genie in a Bottle" was originally called "If You Want to Be With Me." It became a number one hit in 20 countries and was a platinum single in America. Note: Kipner and Frank also scored with the top five smash "The Hardest Thing" by 98 Degrees.

"What a Girl Wants" (written by Guy Roche and Shelly Peiken)
Christina really liked the jazzy, unique structure of the song. It also had that killer hook—"what a girl wants, what a girl needs." Christina is a huge blues fan, and she loved singing the R&B-styled riffs and background parts. The writers-producers both got hot with Brandy's "Almost Doesn't Count" and Meredith Brooks' "Bitch." The song was originally called "What a Girl Needs," but we thought "What a Girl Wants" was catchier.

"I Turn to You" (written by Diane Warren)
Diane is one of the greatest writers in pop music history. She has a legacy of hits with Whitney Houston, Toni Braxton, Celine Dion, LeAnn Rimes, Arrowsmith and just about every super-star there is. Diane was one of the first to recognize Christina's great talent. She personally chose this awesome ballad for Christina. It is one of Christina's favorite songs, and it show-cases her emotional depth and vocal range better than any song on the album. The lyrics speak to the spiritual connection between souls—friends or lovers—in time of need, being there for each other.

"So Emotional" (written by Franne Golde and Tom Snow)
This was submitted as a simple demo produced by newcomer Ron Harris. We liked the demo so much, we converted it into Christina's key and put her voice on the track. The song takes Christina to more of an R&B place. Franne wrote the beautiful Selena ballad "Dreaming," and Tom is a veteran who wrote "He's So Shy" and "Don't Know Much."

"Come On Over" (written by Paul Rein and Johan Aberg)
They say Sweden is the capital of pop, and here's more evidence! This song was sent over from Sweden. We liked the energy of the song and that killer hook, "come on over, come on over, baby!" Christina put her soulful twist on the vocals with producer Aaron Zigman. Here's another one that had a different title: "All I Want Is You." We just kept coming back to "Come On Over," so we changed it!

"Reflection" (written by Matthew Wilder and David Zippel)
Recording this song was the turning point in Christina's career. Right after her audition in New York, I received a call from an old friend, Chris Montan, the head of music for Disney Studios. He was working on their new animated feature, *Mulan,* and was looking for a voice that could record the challenging end-title song, "Reflection." He sent over the demo tape, and I knew immediately it could be a great song for Christina. I called Christina at her home in Wexford, outside of Pittsburgh, PA. "Can you sing the high E above middle C?" I asked. "Can you record it on any old tape recorder and Fed-Ex it to me?" Christina came through with a bathroom rendition of "Run to You," complete with an impressive high E. Soon she was on the next plane to Los Angeles and got the job on the spot! "Reflection" became a well-known radio hit and was nominated for a Golden Globe. The lyrics deal with the impor-tance of inner beauty. The strong message of self-reliance really connected Christina to her fans. The *Mulan* album went double-platinum, and "Reflection" is one of Christina's most beloved songs in concert.

"Love for All Seasons" (written by Carl Sturken and Evan Rogers)
Christina loved the cool and breezy style of the song and became fast friends with Evan and Carl. They got hot and scored a smash with "God Must Have Spent a Little More Time on You" with 'N Sync right before we recorded this song up in Bronxville, New York.

"Somebody's Somebody" (written by Diane Warren)
Another great song, specially written for Christina by Diane Warren. Christina added soul-ful background parts on the intro and outro, giving it her own special flavor. The words express a universal desire, to be "Somebody's Somebody," the importance of feeling need-ed and loved.

"When You Put Your Hands on Me" (written by Robin Thicke and James Gass)
One of Christina's favorites. Robin is a great R&B singer in his own right, and the two of them connected right away. Written specially for Christina, the song celebrates the physical side of attraction and the feelings of "losing control" from powerful love. Robin got hot with the smash hit "Give It to You," which he wrote for Jordan Knight.

"Blessed" (written by Trevon Potts)
Blessed was a song that came on a tape with more than 20 others! Just as we were about to give up, we decided, "okay, one more song." And lo and behold, "Blessed"! It was just the right simple, pretty song we needed to balance out the album. Trevon got hot with his number one hit "Angel of Mine" for Monica.

"Love Will Find a Way" (written by Carl Sturken and Evan Rogers)
Another catchy, up-tempo fun song with a positive message for all young people.

"Obvious" (written by Heather Holley)
"Obvious" was one of the songs on Christina's original demo before she signed with RCA. It's her favorite song on the album, and the most strikingly personal. It's a love story about the fear of rejection and the power of attraction. One of the most inspired melodies of the album, "I don't know what I'm doing anymore . . . I'm feeling like a little girl," Christina belts this out with a total connection to her inner soul. Heather and her boyfriend, producer Rob Hoffman, are two of Christina's best friends and were there at the beginning. When the three of them got together, the results were pure magic.

Christina Aguilera has already stacked up quite a list of accomplishments all in 1999: her number one album; a number one single in 20 countries; millions of record sales around the world; performances on "The Tonight Show" with Jay Leno, "The Late Show" with David Letterman, "Donnie & Marie," "Showtime at the Apollo," "Soul Train" and "Good Morning America"; hosting MTV's "Total Request Live"; performing for President Bill Clinton; appearing on the cover of *Teen People, Teen Celebrity, Latina, Cosmo Girl* and *Arena*; and written about in *The New York Times,* the *Los Angeles Times, The Wall Street Journal, People* magazine, *YM* and *Time* magazine.

She is an artist with staying power—one of the world's freshest and most gifted vocalists, a stylistic trendsetter, video superstar, great entertainer and all-round sweet-normal-fun teenager. I'm proud to have been a part of bringing Christina Aguilera to a worldwide audience that can enjoy her musical gifts, her extraordinary talent and her irrepressible spirit for years to come.

Ron Fair
Senior Vice President, Artists & Repertoire/Executive Producer—RCA Records
Hollywood, California
November 9, 1999

GENIE IN A BOTTLE

Words and Music by
PAMELA SHEYNE, DAVID FRANK
and STEVE KIPNER

Genie in a Bottle - 5 - 1
PF9927

© 1999 APPLETREE SONGS LTD. (PRS) and EMI APRIL MUSIC INC./
STEPHEN A. KIPNER MUSIC/GRIFF GRIFF MUSIC
All Rights for APPLETREE SONGS LTD. Administered in the U.S. and Canada by
WARNER-TAMERLANE PUBLISHING CORP. (BMI)
All Rights Reserved

WHAT A GIRL WANTS

Words and Music by
GUY ROCHE and
SHELLY PEIKEN

Slow, funky groove ♩ = 72

Chorus:

N.C.

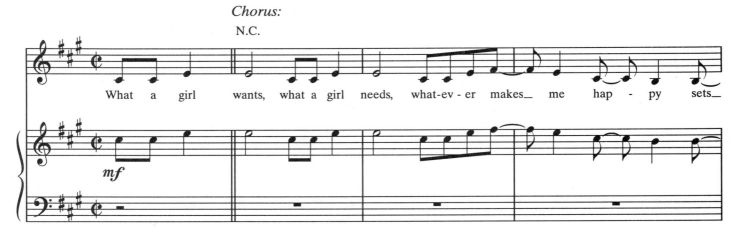

What a girl wants, what a girl needs, what-ev-er makes__ me hap-py sets__

__ you free. What a girl wants, what a girl needs, what-ev-er keeps__ me in__ your arms.__

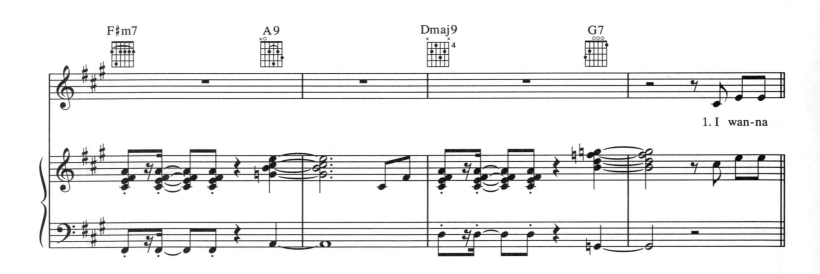

F#m7   A9   Dmaj9   G7

1. I wan-na

What a Girl Wants - 8 - 1
PF9927

© 1999 MAUNITI L.A. (BMI), SUSHI TOO MUSIC (BMI) and HIDDEN PUN MUSIC INC. (BMI)
All Rights for MAUNITI L.A. outside the U.S. and Canada Administered by WARNER-TAMERLANE PUBLISHING CORP.
All Rights Reserved

Chorus:

wants, what a girl needs, what-ev-er makes__ me hap-py sets__ you free,__ and I'm thank-ing you for know-ing ex-act-ly.

Repeat ad lib. and fade

Verse 2:
A weaker man might have walked away, but you had faith,
Strong enough to move over and give me space
While I got it together,
While I figured it out.
They say if you love something, let it go;
If it comes back, it's yours.
That's how you know it's for keeps, yeah, it's for sure,
And you're ready and willin' to give me more than…
(To Chorus:)

I TURN TO YOU

Words and Music by
DIANE WARREN

© 1999 REALSONGS (ASCAP)
All Rights Reserved

Chorus:

SO EMOTIONAL

Words and Music by
FRANNE GOLDE and TOM SNOW

© 1999 FRANNE GEE MUSIC and TOM SNOW MUSIC (BMI)
All Rights for FRANNE GEE MUSIC Administered by WARNER-TAMERLANE PUBLISHING CORP. (BMI)
All Rights Reserved

Chorus:

You make me feel so e-mo-tion-al.___ I

can't let go, I'm so e-mo-tion-al.___ I'm

sink-ing fast in-to an o-cean full of you.___

I'm so e-mo-tion-al.___

2. You take me

Chorus:

You make me feel so e-mo-tion-al.__ I can't let go, I'm

so e-mo-tion-al.__ I'm sink-ing fast in-

Repeat ad lib. and fade

to an o-cean full of you.__ I'm so e-mo-tion-al.__

Verse 2:
You take me high and low, you know.
I'm never sure which way you're gonna go,
You're such a mystery to me.
But, baby, hot or cold, you got a hold
Of my imagination.
I think you know what I mean.
(To Chorus:)

COME ON OVER
(All I Want Is You)

Words and Music by
PAUL REIN and JOHAN ABERG

Moderately fast ♩ = 120

© 1999 AIR CHRYSALIS SCANDINAVIA AB/ECLECTIC MUSIC/MADHOUSE FORLAG AB/BMG PUBLISHING SCANDINAVIA
All Rights for AIR CHRYSALIS SCANDINAVIA in the U.S. and Canada Administered by CHRYSALIS MUSIC (ASCAP)
All Rights Reserved

Verse 2:
I want you to know,
You could be the one for me, yes, you could.
You've got all I'm looking for, you've got personality.
(I know,) I know, (you know,) you know,
I'm gonna give you more.
The things you do,
I've never felt this way before.
So, boy, won't you come,
Won't you come and open my door?
Listen to me.
(To Chorus:)

From the Walt Disney Motion Picture "MULAN"

REFLECTION

Music by MATTHEW WILDER
Lyrics by DAVID ZIPPEL

1. Look at me, you may think you see who I really am, but you'll never know me. Ev'ry day it's as if I play a part.

© 1998 WALT DISNEY MUSIC CO. (ASCAP)
All Rights Reserved   Used by Permission

LOVE FOR ALL SEASONS

Words and Music by
CARL STURKEN and EVAN ROGERS

Moderately slow ♩ = 72

Oh yeah, yeah, oh yeah, yeah, yeah.

Love for All Seasons - 7 - 1
PF9927

© 1999 Songs of Universal, Inc. and Bayjun Beat Music (BMI)
All Rights Controlled and Administered by Songs of Universal, Inc.
All Rights Reserved

1.

2.

Bridge:

Verse 2:
I'll be there for you,
Keepin' you warm through the storm.
I'll guide you, stand by you until the stars fall from the sky.
When you call me, I never hesitate,
Makin' you wait for my love, never lie, love.
It's something that I just can't deny.
I'll read your each and every feelin' when you need me to.
So now I gotta let you know, this love's for you.
(To Chorus:)

SOMEBODY'S SOMEBODY

Words and Music by
DIANE WARREN

Moderately ♩ = 100

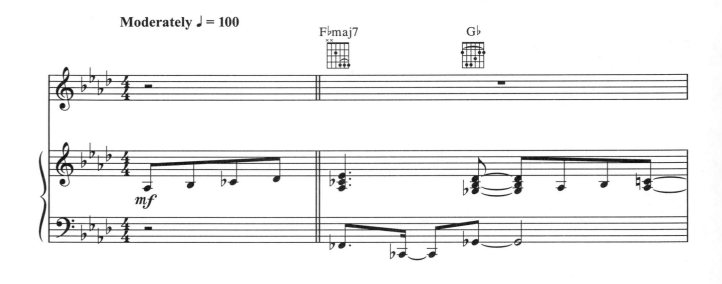

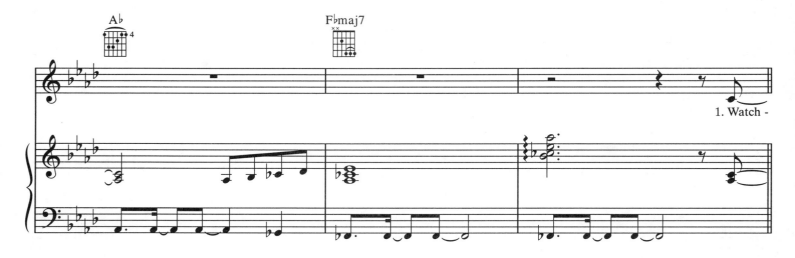

Verse:

in'___ lov - ers walk - in', hand___
ing___ all of my time, spend -

Somebody's Somebody - 7 - 1
PF9927

© 1999 REALSONGS (ASCAP)
All Rights Reserved

Chorus:

WHEN YOU PUT YOUR HANDS ON ME

Words and Music by
ROBIN THICKE and
JAMES GASS

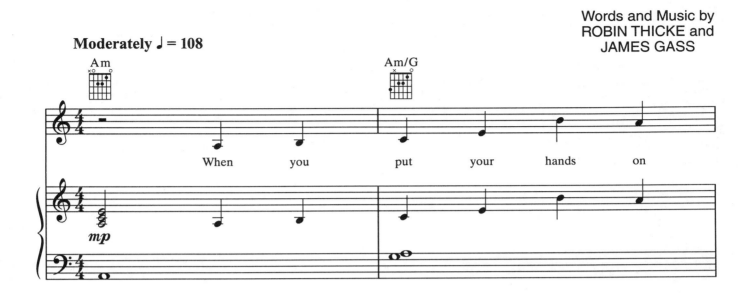

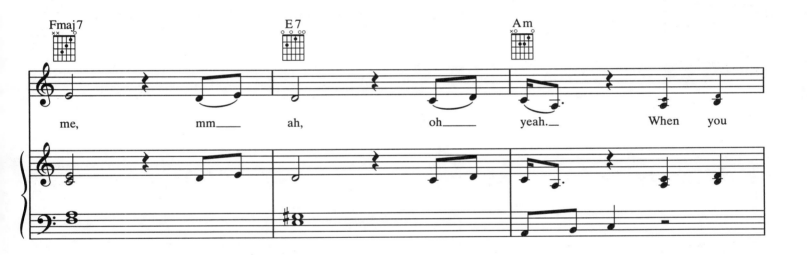

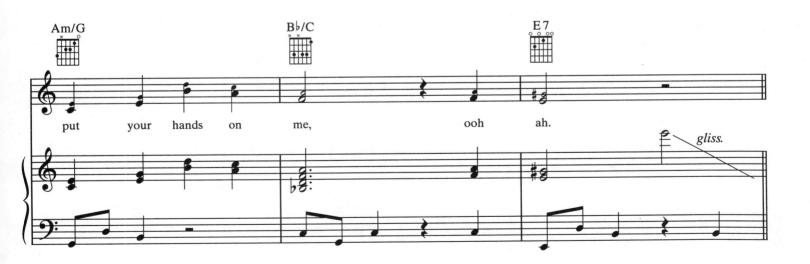

When You Put Your Hands on Me - 5 - 1
PF9927

© 1999 I LIKE 'EM THICKE MUSIC/DA GASS COMPANY MUSIC (ASCAP)
All Rights Reserved   Used by Permission

Verse:

1. I don't know 'bout the trav-el of time and I've nev-er seen most of the world,___
2. *See additional lyrics*

___ ooh.___ I don't know, div-ing out of the sky, or liv-

ing like the dia-monds of pearl,___ ooh.___ See, I have-n't danced_ to a mu-

si-cal tune___ and I have-n't no-ticed the flow-ers in bloom._

Chorus:

Repeat ad lib. and fade

Verse 2:
I don't know if a doll can unwind
Or how to make a person go.
I don't know how to be what you like
And simply open up the depths of my soul.
So I keep my wings and my eyes on the down,
Ready for nothing, but holding my ground.
I haven't used a particular noun very much,
Then we touched.
(To Chorus:)

LOVE WILL FIND A WAY

Words and Music by
CARL STURKEN and EVAN ROGERS

Moderately ♩ = 104

Shoo - doo - doop, doo - doo - doop, doo, doot, doo, doo, doot, doo.

Shoo - doo - doop, doo - doo - doop, doo, doot, doo, doo, doot, doo.

Verse:

1. No one ev - er said that love was gon - na be eas - y._____ Got - ta take the ups and downs, the
2. *See additional lyrics*

© 1999 Songs of Universal, Inc. and Bayjun Beat Music (BMI)
All Rights Controlled and Administered by Songs of Universal, Inc.
All Rights Reserved

Chorus:

No, the rain__ won't last for-ev-er, find a way__ to make it bet-ter. Long as we__ can stand__ to-geth-er,

love__ will find__ a way.__ Gon-na make__ a new to-mor-row, say good-bye__ to tears and sor-row.

Bet-ter lis-ten when__ I say, love__ will find__ a way.__ Shoo-doo-doop, doo-doo-doop,

1.

doo, doot, doo, doo, doot, doo. Shoo-doo-doop, doo-doo-doop, doo, doot, doo, doo, doot, doo.__

Chorus:

Verse 2:
Somebody tried to tell me love won't last forever,
Said it only happens in your wildest dreams.
After all is said and done we're still here together.
Never listened to the lies and jealousy.
(You better stop.)
Don't you let 'em turn you around.
(You better stop.)
Hang on to this love that we've found.
Nothing that they say can stand in our way.
(To Chorus:)

OBVIOUS

Words and Music by
HEATHER HOLLEY

Slowly, with emotion ♩ = 69

(with pedal)

Verse 1:

1. Can you hear it in my voice?____

Was it some-thing I____ let____ slip?____

Does the whole____ world

Obvious - 6 - 1
PF9927

© 1999 POP FUTURE MUSIC (ASCAP)
All Rights Administered by WINDSWEPT MUSIC (ASCAP)
All Rights Reserved

BLESSED

Words and Music by
TRAVON POTTS and BROCK WALSH

Moderately slow ♩ = 92

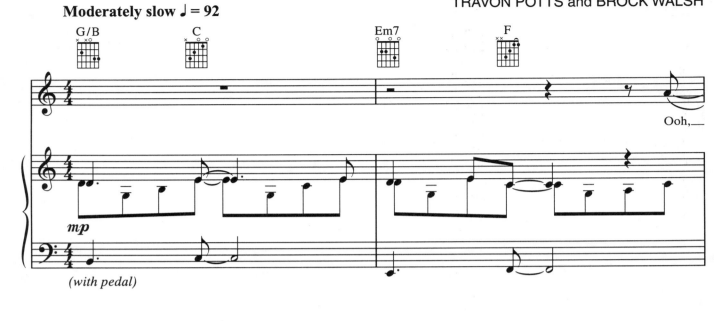

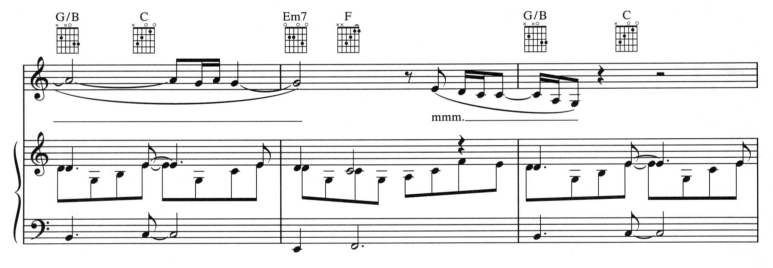

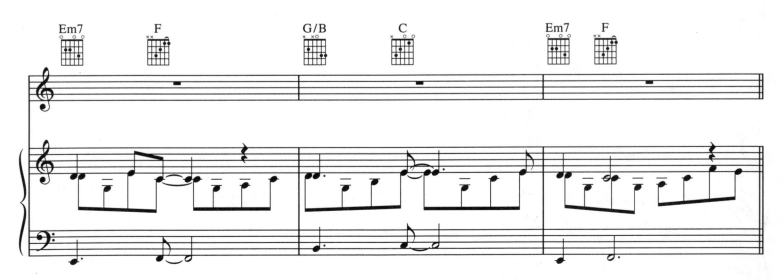

Blessed - 5 - 1
PF9927

© 1999 Travon Music, Motown Tunes and Brock Walsh
All Rights for Travon Music and Motown Tunes Administered by Universal - PolyGram International Publishing, Inc. (ASCAP)
All Rights Reserved

Verse:

1. When I think how life used to be,
2. There are times that test your faith

al - ways walk - ing in the shad - ows.
'til you think you might sur - ren - der.

Then I look_____ at what you've giv - en me;
Ba - by, I'm,_____ I'm not a - shamed to say

I feel like danc - ing on my tip - toes.
that my hopes were grow - ing slen - der.

Bridge:

Deep in - side____ of me,____ you fill me with your gen - tle touch.__

Chorus:

____ You know I'm tru - ly____ blessed__ for ev - 'ry-thing you give__ me,

blessed for all the ten - der - ness you show.____ Do my best__ with

ev - 'ry breath that's in__ me to say you'll nev - er go.____ Nev - er, nev - er, nev - er go._____